My only desire is to spark, or ignite your thoughts...

A GUIDE for THE ENTREPRENEUR

AN INVENTORY of IDEAS FOR WINNING

To order additional copies of this book, contact:
Xlibris Corporation
1-888-795-4274
www.Xlibris.com
Orders@Xlibris.com
53848

A GUIDE *for* THE ENTRE

ALAN DAV

PRENEUR

AN INVENTORY  IDEAS FOR WINNING

ID HIRSCH

acknowledgement

I owe a debt of gratitude to many mentors who have assisted and guided me over the years; however, I need to mention a few special people: My father and brother who were always a source of encouragement, Richard Goldsmith and Ricky Strauss both brilliant and irreverent and both taken way before their time was due, Jack Bemporad who taught me a new way to see the world, Norman King- a true American Original, and Chaim Boyarsky a dedicated teacher.

After a recent lecture at the School of Entrepreneurism at my Alma Mater, the University of Oklahoma, which was well received and appreciated, I decided to compose my thoughts and thus the genesis of this book was born. So a word of thanks to all the faculty and staff at the Price School of Business.

I would also like to acknowledge the stylistic influence of Marshall McLuhan and Quentin Fiore with their ground breaking book The Medium is the Massage and the Meaningful Life Center's Chabad Newsletter, The Week in Review, of which I utilized several parables.

Graphic Design
And
Layout

George J. Abdy, Jr.

dedication

For

Max, Sam & Dylan

pref

'What am I truly capable of achieving' is one of the biggest questions in life. Perhaps as a younger person you had a mentor: a friend, a teacher, a colleague that motivated you to reach great heights. If you did feel blessed, if you didn't, it's hard to describe what you were missing. But all is not lost (1).

Almost daily in my work as a Merchant Banker I work with entrepreneurs. What I realized during the last 25 years is that the same issues and ideas are continually addressed and discussed. The backgrounds, gender, race, religion or ethnic distinctions of entrepreneurs all seem to fade away and a common denominator emerges: Assuming the risk of being your own person and living your life in your own way comes forth.

First and foremost every entrepreneur, not to mention every person in the world connected in business, commerce or human affairs has tackled the thorny issue of success. This guide is a compendium of ideas that will act as a mentor and provide encouragement and perspective for the striving. The inventory of ideas is intended as a resource to enlighten and inform, rather than answer questions, it provides direction. Entrepreneurs are not special people doing special things rather they are ordinary people living in unexpected ways. There will always be the glorious rags to riches story but more often the entrepreneur is a successful small business owner or a manager of a business large or small, a lawyer, an accountant, artist, doctor. ...But their essence is that of a thinker.

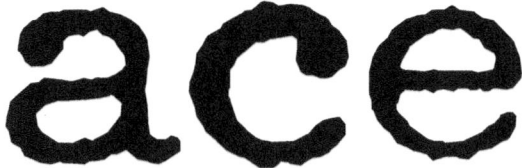

The classic definition of entrepreneur is one who organizes or sets up commercial enterprises to make a profit. But the word is derived from the French entrepreneur "to undertake". An undertaking is a promise or agreement to do something. So being an entrepreneur is essentially a life of assurance; a promise to accept the consequences of risk while living life in a singularly unique manner.

Converting an idea to an operating business is the most difficult part of the entrepreneurial process. It's really 80% of the procedure. The other 20% of the process is developing the operating business into a profitable operating business.

There are so many books, articles, magazines, blogs, web sites, and video sources etc. ad nauseam about success that it has been reduced to a cliché. In most cases the stories and myths in the vernacular are usually the rags to riches tales complete with fairy tale endings. The reality is different, not because most business fail or attain a mammoth market cap, it is that entrepreneurs usually define success in their own terms. This distinction is not unimportant. Living your life in your own individual way is the apex of human freedom.

ENTREPRENEURISM IS NOW A LIFESTYLE: A CHOICE ON HOW TO LIVE ONE'S LIFE AND EXPERIENCE A UNIQUE JOURNEY

Alan David Hirsch

New York City

November 2008

The Lau Tzu states:

" Every journey starts
with a single step "

Every person
therefore
has the
opportunity to
start on their
life's journey.

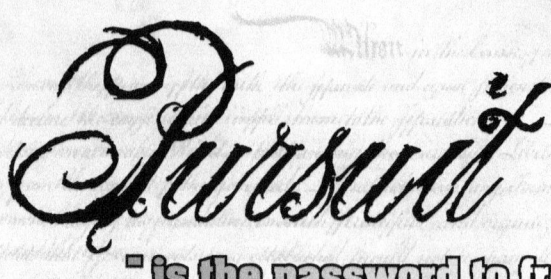
Pursuit is the password to freedom

After you start your journey, keep in mind the wisdom of the Declaration of Independence:

"We hold these truths to be self evident, that all men were created equal, that they are endowed by their Creator with certain inalienable rights, that are among these are, life, liberty and the pursuit of happiness."

But the PURSUIT of happiness, a specific condition for freedom is NOT a guarantee of happiness. In business there is no guarantee of success but once you start on your journey and take that first step, you commence your individual pursuit of happiness and that makes all the difference.

4

All ENTREPRENEURS
have at least this in common:
they all took the first step

Dr. Zira: "What will he find out there doctor?"

Dr. Zaius: "His destiny."

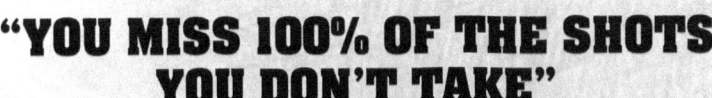

"YOU MISS 100% OF THE SHOTS YOU DON'T TAKE"

- Wayne Gretzky

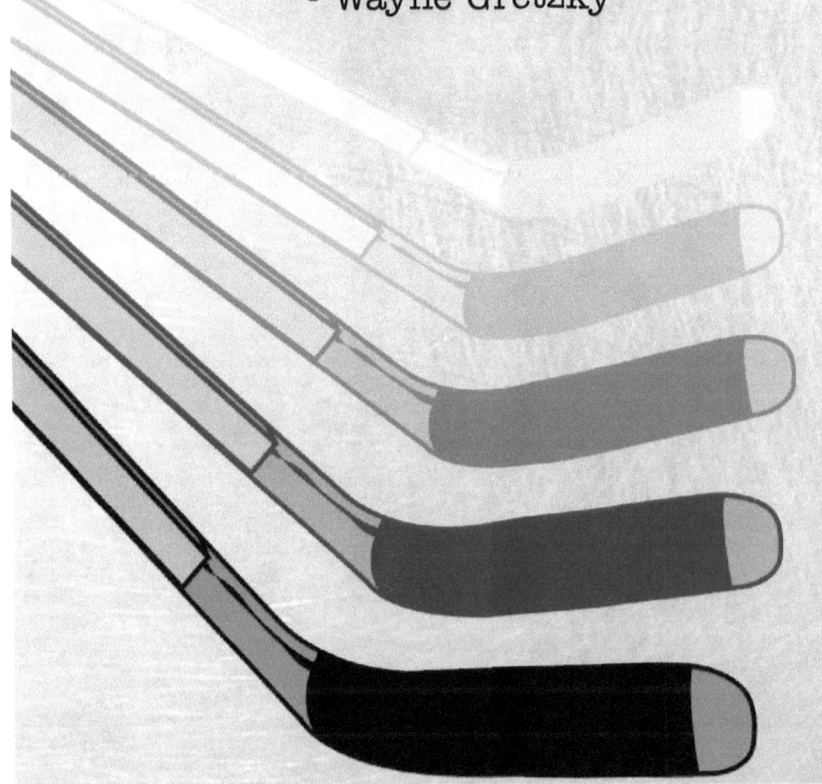

"Twenty years from now you will be more disappointed by the things you didn't do than by the ones you did do."

— Mark Twain

The chances we take...

The greater the happiness, the greater
could be the sadness…
The more exciting the achievement, the
more devastating could be the failure…

These are the chances we take when we
reach for *something worthwhile*

(2)

**Your view of the world and your
own personal definition of success
will indicate whether you are
successful or not.**

For over 3000 years people have grappled
with the question of what should be the
purpose of my life and in what manner should
I live. Before all the self-improvement and
success guru's of the modern business world
explicating their views of success, Aristotle,
Greek Philosopher, 384-322 B.C. noted
student of Plato and one of the greatest minds
of the western intellectual tradition, outlined
some fundamental characteristics of human
behavior. (3,4)

Aristotle adroitly states
that when most people are asked:
What do you want?

They respond in ONE of THREE ways:

We would want money

We would want pleasure

We would want celebrity

**Is this or
some similar derivation
your definition of success?**

**He then outlines the
problem of each of
these answers.**

Simply. If the only satisfaction in life comes from money, if money is the only way to happiness, there will never be enough money to satisfy. If the only satisfaction in life comes from pleasure, if pleasure is the only way to happiness, there will never be enough pleasure to satisfy.

But through
EDUCATION, DISCIPLINE AND TEMPERANCE
we CAN overcome
these all too human traits.

The entrepreneur too must constantly **educate** oneself, be **disciplined** in all aspects of life and act with **temperance**.

Develop a philosophy and a way to see the world.

Winning is great and the desire for riches can be a worthy goal and sometimes is THE measurement of success.

But in order to live your life in your own way you must define your life in your own terms.

"To laugh often and much;
to win the respect of intelligent people
and affection of children; to earn the
appreciation of honest critics and endure
the betrayal of false friends;
to appreciate the beauty, to find the best in others;
to leave the world a bit better, whether by a
healthy child, a garden patch or a
redeemed social condition; to know even
one life has breathed easier because you
have lived. This is to have succeeded."

– Ralph Waldo Emerson

What type of life should one strive for?

This is an age-old question.
From the beginning of civilization people
have queried what is the best kind of life?

What type of life should I live?

AND
are these values relevant
in the world you live in?

When **Maria Bartiromo**, host of CNBC's *Closing Bell* asked **George Soros**,

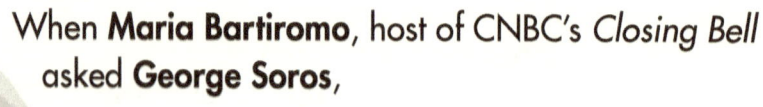

"Why have you become so political?"

He responded,

"I was a human being before I became a Hedge Fund manager."

G. SOROS

the Labor of Life

"Man was born to toil," says the verse- a fact of human nature readily affirmable by asking yourself a simple question: How many happy retirees do I know?

That nothing worthwhile comes easy in life- that, indeed, anything that does come easy is ultimately spurned as worthless- is God's greatest gift to man. For it is this twist of human nature that enables us to experience achievement and fulfillment in our endeavors.

Chassidim (righteous person) would illustrate this point with the following story:

A wealthy nobleman was once touring his estate and came upon a peasant pitching hay. The nobleman was fascinated by the flowing motions of the peasant's arms and shoulders and the graceful sweep of the pitchfork through the air. He so greatly enjoyed the spectacle that he struck a deal with the peasant: for ten rubbles a day, the peasant agreed to come to the mansion and display his hay-pitching technique in the nobleman's drawing room.

The next day, the peasant arrived at the mansion, hardly concealing his glee at his new line of "work." After swinging his empty pitchfork for an hour, he collected his ten rubbles- many times his usual take for a week backbreaking labor. But by the following day, his enthusiasm had somewhat waned. Before the week was out, he announced that he was quitting his commission.

"I don't understand," puzzled the nobleman. "Why would you rather swing heavy loads outdoors in the winter cold and the summer heat, when you can perform an effortless task in the comfort of my home and earn many times your usual wages?"

"But master," said the peasant. "I don't see the work."(5)

Equilibrium is important especially when epiphany is elusive and occasional

We can learn about life's peaks and valleys from **Robert Hunter** who wrote one of the most often quoted lines in rock history from the Grateful Dead song 'Truckin':

> Sometime the light's all shining on me
> Other times I can barely see
> Lately it's occurred to me
> What a long strange trip it's been...

David Dobbs (6) in his thematic essay Light and Dark in the Lyrics of Robert Hunter states all too clearly...

We humans spend our lives bumbling along, and occasionally we have moments of insight, or of grace. They don't last long, but they somehow make life more worth living. Many writers have attempted to capture this feeling of momentary magical thinking; religions are founded upon seeking a permanent state of illumination or grace...

The light. Robert Hunter's lyrics for the Grateful Dead make repeated allusion to the gold ring of understanding, knowledge, bliss, grace, or whatever else "it" might be called, which all too often just slips away when we try to reach it. It's a transitory thing, this "knowing."

Hunter uses evocations of light and dark, of day and night, to present many shades of meaning. Dawn and dark can be seen as birth and death, as well as knowing and unknowing. And they are not completely separate at all times: sometimes there is only grey. Sometimes the darkness gives birth to the light, as mystery and the unknown are as necessary as revelation...

It's a dichotomy as old as every creation story, or as told as Adam and Eve and their apple. And there is the final, terrifying truth that "the more you know, the more you know the less you know." But it's the occasional moment of enlightenment, of transcendence, that makes all the bumbling about worthwhile.

For the entrepreneur
either everything seems to work seamlessly
[the light]

OR

There are serious impediments to goals
[darkness]

Some day's you wake up and you have tremendous
clarity and other days you could be seeing a wall...
modulate these extremes.

On occasion when watching a football game, I often see after a touchdown is scored a **"victory dance"** where the person scoring walks around like a chicken or dances as if praying for rain. When the same player fumbles or commits some other **"mistake"** they often overtly walk around the field sulking or shaking his head. Remember this analogy. If you score a touchdown act like you've been in the end zone before and when you fumble remember that this is part of the game also.

Modulate these extremes...

In a world of individual differences create and develop your own self-guidance and improvement scenario.

But each and every entrepreneur should be aware that the world of rugged American Individualism and idealism and the notion that one can create their own world (and much more) is rooted in the American Philosophy of Ralph Waldo Emerson and Henry David Thoreau. Known as the Transcendentalist Movement these American thinkers were the original "self actualize" or "do your own thing" people.

One might find it an odd juxtaposition, providing guidance for Entrepreneurs, while asking them to develop a philosophy of life rooted in Transcendentalism- a way to live one's life in a manner that puts the spiritual understanding above brash naked capitalism.

But this uniquely American philosophy is ironically the unintended foundation for modern entrepreneurs.

By TRANSCENDING an ordinary way of thinking you develop a unique way of seeing and CREATE your own environments. Emerson states clearly, "What I must do is all that concerns me, not what people think..."

Transcendentalism

The fundamental world view of religion...

The spiritual aspect of nature- in effect the first environmental movement...

Literature- and the voice of the individual...

Education...

The idea of Civil Disobedience. The first anti-war movement...

Artists, Musicians, and Painters...

Politics and Race relations and civil rights...

It's influence is still felt today...

So create and devise a plan
since all self-improvement plans

1. Financial / Material success

2. Physical condition:
   staying in shape and good health

KNOWING IS COMING TO
THE

UNDERSTANDING IS HOW
TO

SELF KNOWLEDGE IS
THE BEDROCK
ENTREPRENEURIAL

YOU CAN
REINVENT
YOU ARE

that works for you...
address these 4 categories:

3. Psychological and emotional well-being

4. Spiritual understanding

TERMS WITH
GENERAL IDEA.

THIS IDEA RELATES
YOU.

OF ALL
EFFORTS.

THE WHEEL BECAUSE
THE WHEEL.

the TASTE of MUSIC

"A blessing is like rain," Rabbi Israel Baal Shem Tov taught. When rain is preceded by plowing and sowing, and followed with reaping and harvesting, it yields abundant fruit; otherwise, it achieves nothing. Likewise, a person can be granted the greatest gifts from Above, but unless he makes himself a fit vessel to receive them, unless he learns to appreciate and utilize them properly, they are but futile rain on a barren field.

Chassidim (righteous person) would illustrate this point with the following story:

A king once decided to reward a peasant who had done him a great service. "Shall I give him a sack of gold? A bag of pearls?" thought the king. "But these mean virtually nothing to me. I want, for once, to truly give something- something that I will miss, a gift that constitutes a sacrifice for me."

Now this king had a nightingale who sang the sweetest songs a human ear had ever heard. He treasured the nightingale over all else, and literally found life. unbearable without it. So he summoned the peasant to his palace and gave him the bird.

"This," said the king, "is in appreciation for your loyalty and devotion."

"Thank you, Your Majesty," said the peasant, and took the royal gift to his humble home.

A while later, the king was passing through the peasant's village and commanded his coachman to halt at the peasant's door. "How are you enjoying my gift?" he inquired of his beloved subject.

"The truth to tell, Your Majesty," said the peasant, "the bird's meat was quite tough- all but inedible, in fact. But I cooked it with lots of potatoes, and it gave the stew an interesting flavor."

(7)

BUSINESS PLANS
and
RAISING CAPITAL

"When someone asks you for the time, don't
give them the history of the watch"

— **Norman King**

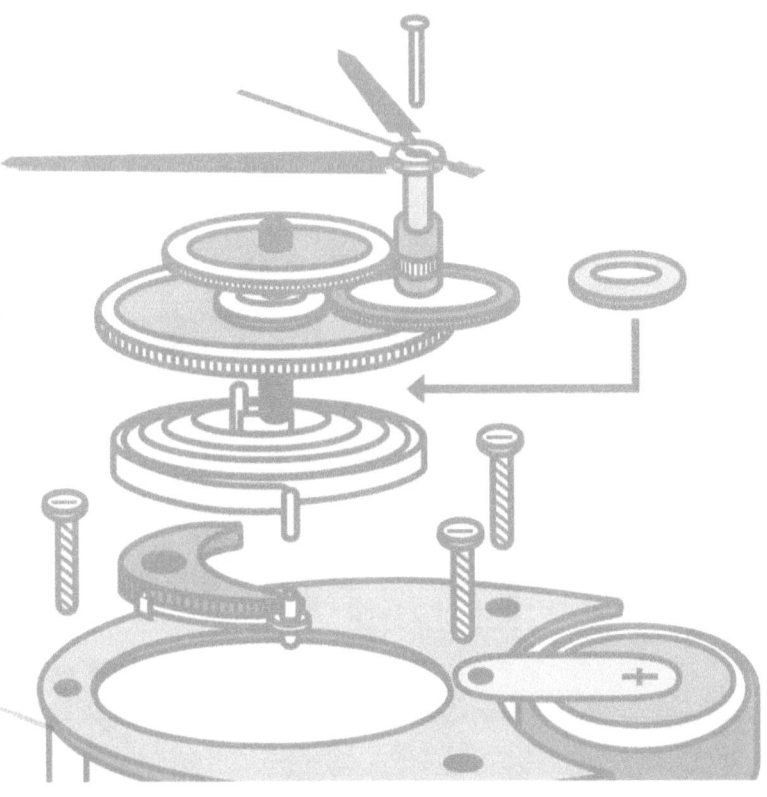

At some point in our education, usually at the elementary or middle school level, most of us have taken a course in Journalism. We have to learn how to write and analyze a newspaper article. We learn that the fundamental tenets of such an article or story contain the answers to **the following questions:**

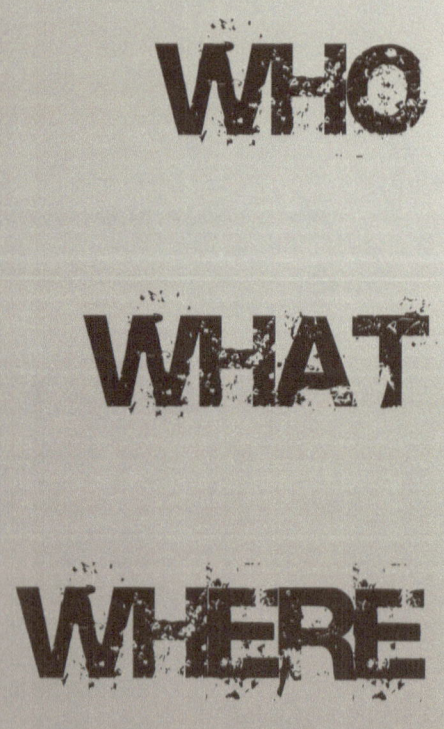

WHO

WHAT

WHERE

 **WHY**

 **WHEN**

AND **HOW**

Any abstract, business plan, summary, term sheet etc. should address **these basic questions.** You will be surprised how many do not. If this seems simplistic it is!

WHO

THE QUESTION

A QUESTION ABOUT

ARE YOU?

ABOUT WHO
IS ALWAYS
THE QUESTIONER.

What's it

WHAT ARE YOU

WHAT IS

all about?

DOING?
YOUR BUSINESS
AND
YOUR CUSTOMERS.

THIS HAPPENING?

WHY

TELL ME WHY
WE SHOULD
BE INVOLVED

INVEST, FUND OR WITH YOU.

WHEN IS

THIS HAPPENING?

AND HOW
IS THIS GOING

A True

...I recall at a pitch meeting on a company that we were considering acquiring where I had thought I had everything figured out. Spreadsheets were abounding, yellow pads everywhere and I made my presentation. I even figured out how to finance the transaction 125% with outside financing. Then the first question was asked,

Little Story...

"How are we going to make money with this company?" "With only a 21% gross margin it will be tough if not nearly impossible" I figured everything out except the "HOW" I thought to myself how ironic; I did not follow my own advice. Either the cosmic sense of humor changed or I've gone crazy...

Do Start-Ups Really Need Formal

By Kelly K. Spors
(truncated version)

Business schools and consultants have long preached that writing a formal business plan greatly improves a start up's odds of success. But a growing number of academics are questioning whether that's really the case.

Budding entrepreneurs can spend months, sometimes years, polishing elaborate 50 to 100 page business plans that include financial projections, market research, and intricate details on day-to-day planning and organization. But skeptics say there's little concrete evidence that extensive planning is highly correlated to success...

...The most compelling reason to write a formal business plan, even critics agree, is when seeking venture capital or angel investors. But only roughly 55,000 of about four million start-ups each year get that money. And even then, the merits of having a lengthy business plan may be overblown.

'Just Do It'

"What we really don't want to do is literally spend a year or more essentially writing a business plan without knowing we have actual customers," says William Bygrave, an entrepreneurship professor at Babson College in Wellesley, Mass., who says he generally advocates "just do it."

Entrepreneurs must be nimble, and will be more apt to stick with a flawed concept they spent months drafting, he adds.

The doubts fly in the face of a huge, lucrative business-planning industry, cock full of authors writing step-by-step guides and consultants selling business-planning services. A recent search for "business plan" on Amazon.com turned up more than 19,000 book titles. Business schools also have reason to push planning: It's much easier to teach than intuition...

...A study recently released by Babson College analyzed 116 businesses started by alumni who graduated between 1985 and 2003. Comparing success measures such as annual revenue, employee numbers and net income, the study found no statistical difference in success between those businesses started with formal written plans and those without them. The study concludes that "unless you need to raise external start-up capital from institutional sources or business angel investors, you do not need to write a formal business plan."

Amar Bhide, a Columbia University entrepreneurship professor,

ET JOURNAL

Business Plans?

Thursday, January 9, 2007

found that 41% of Inc. Magazine's 1989 list of the 500 fastest-growing private firms didn't have business plans and 26% had only rudimentary plans. A follow-up by the magazine in 2002 found the numbers without a plan have remained pretty much the same. Many business concepts are "transitional in nature," meaning there are competitive advantages to starting the business quickly and by the time you write a full business plan "the opportunity will be gone."

...Scott Shane, a professor at Case Western Reserve University, says most studies that discount business-planning are flawed because they don't correct for business failure rates, only accounting for businesses that survived. If they did, they would find that a far greater number of businesses that failed never had a formal business plan. Mr. Shane's research controls for failure rates and shows that businesses with formal business plans are more likely to survive. He says most business ideas don't have to be rushed to market and that it typically takes a long time for businesses to get started anyway. "I'm not sure that saying, "Oh, people

shouldn't write business plans' would accelerate a lot more people into the start-up process," he says. "they seem to be held back by a lot of other things."

...Tim Petersen, managing director of Arboretum Ventures, a health-care venture-capital firm in Ann Arbor, Mich. says he generally prefers getting 5 to 10 page summaries of business ideas or PowerPoint presentations over lengthy business plans.

"I'll have to confess, it's not always crucial to have the 60-page business plan," he says. While most entrepreneurs seeking should have their ideas well-formulated, "some people will get a little caught up in the perfection of their plan," he says.

Even some believers of business planning say formal planning foes have some valid points. Tom Kinnear, executive director of the entrepreneurial studies institute at the University of Michigan says writing a business plan shouldn't take more than 3 or 4 weeks.

"There's no question that some people are obsessed with writing plans that are too wrought with detail," Mr. Kinnear says. "Early on, all you really need is a compass." (7)

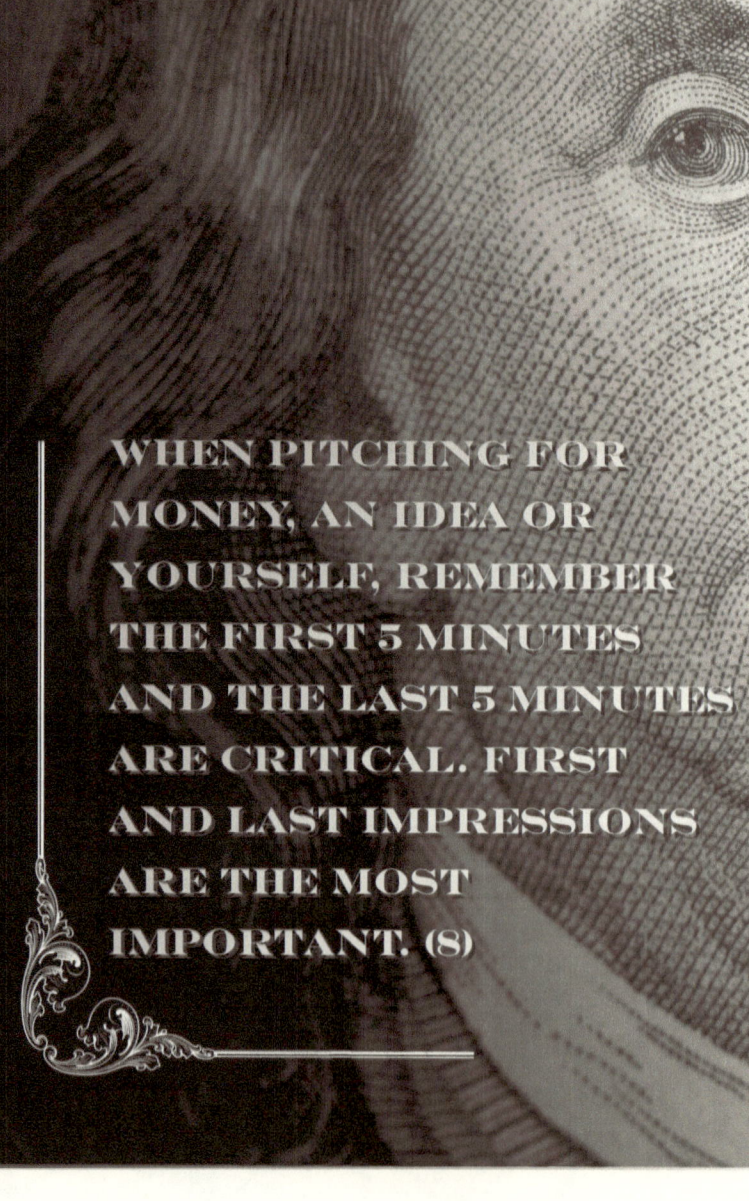

WHEN PITCHING FOR MONEY, AN IDEA OR YOURSELF, REMEMBER THE FIRST 5 MINUTES AND THE LAST 5 MINUTES ARE CRITICAL. FIRST AND LAST IMPRESSIONS ARE THE MOST IMPORTANT. (8)

THE FIRST FIVE

☑ Appearance matters. Be who you are but look your best.

☑ Remember to use your elevator pitch. In essence imagine two people walk into an elevator and one person asks the other, what do you do? You need to answer before the car reaches its destination. In Hollywood, as depicted in the movie The Player, the maxim is: Pitch me the movie in 25 words or less. This should be the rule for all entrepreneurs so keep it simple...

MINUTES:

- ✅ Listen; really listen- simple questions require simple answers.

- ✅ It is commonly known by trial lawyers that most juries decide the case usually during the opening statements... the pitch runs along parallel lines... many opinions are formed during the first meeting, in fact during the first several minutes of conversation... a strong opening is critical.

THE LAST FIVE MINUTES:

✔ In the context of the meeting-
what are you trying to
accomplish? Prepare for a
successful close.

✔ Learn to expect objections AND learn to
overcome objections. Only a closer can
overcome objections.

Objections fall into three categories:

Psychological Hedges

Valid Objections

Irrevocable Objections

Psychological Hedges

Temporary hesitations or questions or even excuses. These require quick responses. Typical examples of a psychological hedge (in selling) is when you enter any retail store and the salesperson asks, "Can I help you?" the first objection / answer / psychological hedge is the answer, "No. I'm just looking." In closing a pitch meeting it's typical to hear," I'm not sure we're interested in this sector." "Let me think about it." Closers overcome these instantly.

Valid Objections

These are real and serious objections that must be addressed as succinctly as possible. Perhaps your talking with a venture capitalist and you should be discussing your project with a hedge fund or strategic partner. The deal is not priced right. These are valid objections and you must overcome them by answering them directly and determine if they have significant merit or if they are simply a roadblock.

Irrevocable Objections

These are usually fatal. Be prepared to walk and deal with at a later time.

WHAT'S IN
THE FIRST FIVE MINUTES

WHO

WHAT

WHERE

BETWEEN
AND THE LAST FIVE MINUTES?

AND **HOW**

And
REMEMBER
no
WHAT ANYBODY

It s not about the money;

it s just about

matter
TELLS YOU:

the money.

When someone tells you:

That they're suing for the principle....

They like your idea, but they don't invest in start-ups....

We only buy stocks over $5.00...

My spouse won't let me do this deal....

I want to move forward but the committee rejected it...

Whatever;
its ALWAYS about the money

Intangibles provide the pathway to the possible. The tangible or the measurable is what we commonly perceive as the normal way to process the business transaction. Net tangible assets are the basic currency of all financial transactions. But it's the intangibles that often indicate what's really going on or where you're headed.

The transaction or the DEAL is the most routine part of the entrepreneurial life; one is always trying to determine how the deal is going on track or not. Good or bad? Yes or no? But it's almost always the intangible that can provide an insight into the status of the deal.

The tangible are the words or contracts or commitment letters—but the flow of a transaction or how the other party is responding to you can tell you much more about your deal than you might imagine. For instance the "words' you are being told is "everything's fine" or "we're closing next month" but how is this person treating you can indicate what's really happening within the transaction. When someone doesn't call you back, or does not keep their word or does more than what's expected this can be more telling than what they are saying at any given moment.

Look how you are being **treated:**

Are you kept waiting in the lobby for a long time?

Does the person take phone calls during a meeting, and if so by whom?

Decency should be the rule not the exception. When indecency, no matter how dire the situation, is in the open, this is a telling trait of the person, entity or institution.

What is on the person's office walls or credenza?

What's important to them?

THESE INTANGIBLES CAN PROVIDE INSIGHT INTO HOW A PERSON THINKS AND HOW YOU WILL BE TREATED.

One must constantly see the intangible VALUE in everyday life. For instance almost every meeting you take is a possibility. Meetings create another chance at something. Many businesspeople have a certain and specific objective when they take a meeting. This is the tangible. We're raising capital so we're taking various meetings with investors. But the meetings produce zero tangible results. No capital was raised. Logic would dictate that these meetings were a failure. But there are many INTANGIBLE results that go often unnoticed: Connections were created, ideas discussed, future potential foundations were formed. More often than not these future possibilities become fruitful.

INSIGHT:

Each moment in time is filled with possibilities. In each moment we have the power to create real change. Yet, there are distinct moments in history when a window of opportunity opens up - a crack that can catapult us to a new place.

These cracks are rare. And even when they open, they quickly close, precipitated by the complacency that quickly returns.

Change, you will always find, is in direct disproportion to the reverie of apathy.

When an opportunity comes your way, grab it. Because once the moment passes and life returns to normal; you will surely forget. (9)

LUCK AND TIMING DICTATES ALL

INC. Magazine asked its Entrepreneur of the Year the following question:

What is the most overrated skill for an entrepreneur?

The most overrated skill is skill. Luck is more important. The entrepreneur gets credit for being this genius, when really he was just at the right place at the right time (10).

Never underestimate luck. Of course talent, hard work and perseverance are the predicate for luck-good and bad, without the predicate luck could not come into play.

But consider these examples ...

Nikolas Tesla a scientist, futurist and creator actually "invented" many of the ideas that led to commercialism of electricity yet it is Thomas Edison, through hard work, perseverance and fantastic timing who was the inventor of record. But despite a strong mythology as an industrialist, Thomas Edison often failed to capitalize on his inventions. He was famous, but not wealthy. He never commercialized many of his inventions. He often moved from one project to the next prior to bringing the first to a successful commercial venture. Edison was heavily in debt to Henry Ford who as his patron really sustained him. Others commercialized many of Edison's most well known inventions to great financial success.

Both companies, **Microsoft** and **Apple** had similar technologies at the beginning of the information age. The history is well known. Yet Microsoft, who only had a license for the operating system decided to market it as the least expensive for the IBM PC. A smart move but luck dictated that Microsoft was at the right place at the right time and explosive growth was immanent... ironically Apple invented the iPod, which was a derivative idea of the old SONY Walkman.... people walking around with portable music was nothing new... but luck and timing put the iPod front and center....

Before **GOOGLE** there was **GO TO** (which was profitable and had a market cap of $1 Billion), but the market was not ready for an Internet search engine, the early GO TO pioneers realized the need but it appears that they were too early... when GOOGLE entered the market it in essence captured the search engine zeitgeist and the rest is history....

In each of these situations talent, hard work and perseverance paved the way for each lucky situation...

Even "bad" luck isn't what it seems to be. Bad luck, or temporary misfortune or setback is not always bad... Sometimes people fall on hard times and almost immediately thereafter create their most important idea or enterprise.

Richard Kinder, chief executive officer of Kinder Morgan, founded the firm in 1997, before that, he was president at Enron Corp. He left that company when then-Chairman Kenneth Lay declined to make him CEO. {Source Wall Street Journal June 3, 2006).

Lloyd Blankfein, now the Chairman of Goldman Sachs Group, who received one of the largest bonuses in Wall Street history, was actually rejected for a job by the firm. He later landed a job at a trading company, which was ultimately acquired by Goldman...

WITH LUCK AND TIMING

REMEMBER THIS:

"Truth is stranger than fiction because fiction has to be plausible."

— Aldous Huxley

ENTREPR
IS A
THINKING OF AND

"The major advances in civilization societies in which they occur."

— Alfred North Whitehead

ENEURISM
WAY
SEEING
WORLD

are processes that all but wreck the

*Thank you Professor McLuhan

ECONOMICS IS A WAY OF THINKING AND SEEING THE WORLD

THE ECONOMIST
THE BIG
THE WHOLE

THAT IS NOT TO SAY THAT SOME
ORIENTED OR SOME ECONOMISTS

BOTH ENTREPRENEURISM AND
REQUIRE A WILLINGNESS TO
THEORIES AND LOGICAL
FACTS AND STATISTICAL
LESSONS
EVEN

THE ENTREPRENEUR VIEWS THE MICRO, THE INDIVIDUAL
PICTURE, A SMALL PART OF THE ECOSYSTEM, OR THE TREE.

VIEWS THE MACRO,
PICTURE,
GESTALT OR THE FOREST.

ENTREPRENEURS ARE BIG PICTURE
STUDY MICRO ECONOMIC ISSUES.

THE STUDY OF ECONOMICS
COMBINE MANY ELEMENTS:
DEDUCTIONS,
EVIDENCE,
OF HISTORY,
PHILOSOPHY (11)

ONE UNIVERSE

BUT

TWO

WORLDS

THEY BOTH
Understand the importance of trade-offs.

trade (trād), *n.* commerce; exchange of
   goods; buying and selling for gain; a special craft or those engaged in it, as the
   building *trade;* a bargain or swap.

trademark (trād' märk), *n.* a symbol regis-
   tered with the Government to distinguish
   and protect a line of goods or some particu-
   lar product.

trade-off (trād'-ôf), *v.* giving up one advantage
   in order to gain another. For example, a trade off
   may be realized by taking financial loss in order
   to gain a tax deduction that will lower total tax
   liability.

trade price (trād prĭs), the cost of goods to
   the retailer buying from a wholesaler.

trader (trād' ĕr), *n.* one who engages in
   commerce.

trade union (trād ūn' yun), *n.* an organized
   combination of workers engaged in the same
   craft, promoting their common interests.

Entrepreneurs live with same issues as economists, whether macro or micro, except they experience them from a different perspective. A parallel universe would be an apt description.

Economics, although imbued with the language of mathematics and utilizing structural models that sometimes are difficult to access, is ultimately a science about people.

Entrepreneurs are people who experience economic theory in a first person point of view. Ultimately it's about that person and their knowledge. All knowledge is derived from experience and your unique entrepreneurial experience creates specialized knowledge. That is why some many success stories are in conveyed by autobiography. It is their approach, knowledge and insights, in effect their philosophy, that we want to glean the most salient facts. That philosophy is in other words intellectual autobiography...

That person carries within a new way of seeing. This uniqueness is the core of the entrepreneurial experience. This experience commences in the abstract yet has implications in the practical and commercial world. The abstract is the vision. The practical and commercial is the operating business.

Transforming the vision into an operating business is the most demanding and difficult part of the entrepreneurial climb just as utilizing an abstract economic theory in a beneficial practical application is the crux for the economist.

New ways of seeing require a heightened sense of perception... or in other words a new or different intelligence. This new intelligence and perception is more important than I.Q.

(12)

"Millions saw the apple fall,
but Newton was the one who asked why."

-Bernard Baruch

ENTREPR
ARE
ALLEGO
ROCK
OF THE 21ST

ENEURS
THE
RICAL
STARS
CENTURY

Growing up everyone wanted to be a rock star. We all started bands and practiced in our basements, rec rooms and garages. "THE" cultural icons were Elvis, Chuck Berry, Janis Joplin and the Rolling Stones, or just about any favorite band or singer.

Because...

Music was MORE than the music...

Rock and Roll Music- An art form that spoke for a generation, was critically acclaimed, accepted by all and was profitable!

Our current day cultural icons
are better recognized
by the logos that represent them.
... and they too have this in common.

-Just to name a few-

Bill Gates, Donald Trump, Steve Jobs, Oprah Winfrey,

Google founders Larry Page and Sergey Brin,

You Tube founders Chad Hurley and Steve Chen.

In the 21st century it will **"I want to be the next** rather **"I'm going to**

There are many reasons for this chiefly that in the 1950's and 60's rock music was an emerging art form and as it developed and matured, as did its audience, it became more mainstream. As rock aged it mellowed and the anti-establishment became the establishment. Rock did change the world but in the post-modified reality even Bono has his own private equity fund...

be more common to hear
You Tube"
than
be a rock 'n roller"...

**Bono has his own
private equity fund of $1.2 Billion**

82

Business today
[even with an occasional scandal]

is respectable
and
iconoclastic and
Creativity is no longer

The entrepreneur has the opportunity to meld the creative and material worlds and effect positive change within our universe...

In effect entrepreneurs are...

THE ALLEGORICAL ROCK STARS

emanating status.
the domain of the artist.

OF THE 21ST CENTURY.

To make the future is highly risky. It is less risky, however, than not to try and make it...

– Peter Drucker

References

1. The Week In Review, Published by the Meaningful Life Center, Brooklyn, NY, 2006.

2. Freddie Mittman as quoted in the Employee Newsletter.

3. Great Books, Aristotle, Encyclopedia Britannica.

4. Great Authors of the Western Literary Tradition, Part 4, Professor Hertzberg, The Teaching Company.

5. The Week In Review, Published by the Meaningful Life Center, Brooklyn, NY, 2006.

6. David Dodd, Light and Dark in the Lyrics of Robert Hunter, A thematic essay for The Annotated Grateful Dead Lyrics.

7. Wall Street Journal, January 9, 2007, by Kelly K. Spors: 'Do Start-Ups Really Need Formal Business Plans?'

8. Norman King, The First 5 minutes, The Last 5 minutes; Prentice Hall Press, NY 1987.

9. The Week In Review, Published by the Meaningful Life Center, Brooklyn, NY, 2006.

10. Inc. Magazine, 2006.

11. Economics, 3rd Edition, Timothy Taylor, The Teaching Company.

12. Daniel Pink, A Whole New Mind, Riverhead Books, New York, 2005.

Photo References

PAGE 5-6: Planet of the Apes. Courtesy of 20th Century Fox.

PAGE 18: George Soros: World Trade Organization Symposium on Issues Confronting the World Trade System, WTO Headquarters, Geneva, 6-7 July 200.

PAGE 68-69: Data courtesy Marc Imhoff of NASA GSFC and Christopher Elvidge of NOAA NGDC. © Image by Craig Mayhew and Robert Simmon, NASA GSFC.

Essential Reading

Napoleon Hill; Think and Grow Rich

Stephen Covey; The 7 Habits of Highly Effective People

Daniel Pink; A Whole New Mind

Peter Drucker; The Daily Drucker or The Essential Drucker

...the rest is up to YOU.

(and KNOW that YOU DON'T KNOW)

www.ingramcontent.com/pod-product-compliance
Lightning Source LLC
Chambersburg PA
CBHW022111170526
45157CB00004B/1583